Horse&Pony Care

WRITTEN BY
Sandy Ransford

PHOTOGRAPHED BY
Bob Langrish

KINGFISHER

The publisher would like to thank Justine Armstrong-Smith for the use of her yard and show ponies, and the Talland School of Equitation, England, and Hartpury College, England, for their invaluable help in the production of this book.

KINGFISHER

First published 2002 by Kingfisher
an imprint of Macmillan Children's Books
a division of Macmillan Publishers Limited
The Macmillan Building, 4 Crinan Street,
London, N1 9XW
Basingstoke and Oxford
Associated companies througout the world
www.panmacmillan.com

Consultant: Nikki Herbert BHSI

ISBN 978-0-7534-0773-8

10 9 8 7 6 5 4 3 2 1
1TR/0808/TWP/CG(CLSN)/150SMA

A CIP catalogue record for this book is available from the British Library.

Printed in Singapore

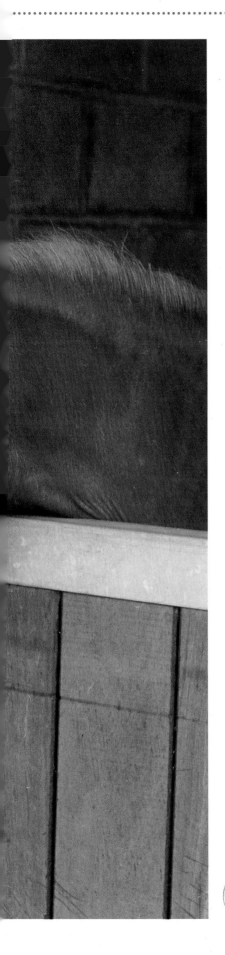

Contents

Keeping a pony

Keeping and looking after a pony is a serious commitment. It is hard work, and takes up a lot of your time. It is also exciting, rewarding – and great fun!

Providing company

Horses and ponies are herd animals and do not like being on their own. They are happiest when living with other horses and ponies, but if this is not possible, then the company of other animals is a good substitute. If you have to keep a pony on his own, visit him frequently and make him feel he is part of family life.

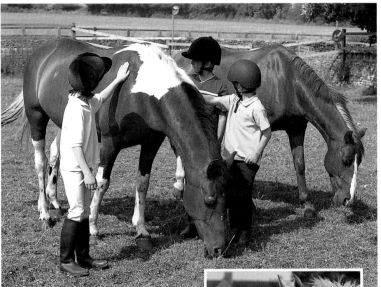

Human contact

Ponies like human company and will always appreciate your visits, though you may not be important enough to them to stop them grazing! Take care they do not tread on your feet as they walk forwards. If you do offer titbits, make sure there are enough to go round all the ponies in the group.

Ponies always enjoy a treat, but they will be pleased to see you even if you visit empty-handed as long as you talk to them and pat them.

Animal companionship

Once they get to know each other and realize they are part of a group that lives together, most animals become friends. Horses and ponies get on well with a variety of animals, from cats and dogs to farm stock.

Although one horse or pony in a group is always dominant, two horses kept together usually become firm friends.

Horses and cats get on well. A cat is a good companion for a pony in the stable or out.

A friendly goat is good company for a lonely horse or pony, as are farm animals such as cattle and sheep.

Regular exercise

If a pony is kept in a stable he must be exercised every day. If it is not possible to ride him, then he should be turned out in the field for a while, or lunged. Exercise keeps the pony fit. His circulation, heart and lungs function better, and his bones and muscles are kept strong and healthy.

What a pony needs

A pony needs food and water, shelter from the weather, regular exercise and companionship. In his natural state, all these things are part of the life that he leads. But when we domesticate horses and ponies and make them work for us, they depend on us to fulfil all these needs. We owe it to them to do this as well as we possibly can.

Some form of shelter

A pony that lives out in a field needs some kind of shelter from sun and flies in summer, and rain, wind and snow in winter. Trees and thick hedges provide a certain amount of protection, but a specially built field shelter is the best solution if it is possible.

Grazing in the field

Every pony should have access to good grazing for at least part of each day. This is his natural way of life. Giving him the freedom to graze, move from place to place, roll and occasionally gallop around, helps to keep him calm.

A suitable stable

If the pony is to be stabled, the building must meet certain requirements. The doorway should be high enough so he cannot bang his head. The stable should be light, with plenty of ventilation. It should have good drainage, so that the bedding stays as dry as possible.

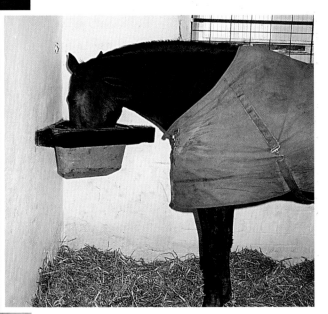

Feeding routine

A stabled pony needs regular feeding. The amount of food he needs depends on the individual and the amount of work he is being asked to do, but all stabled ponies need hay to replace the grass they would eat if they lived out in a field and grazed.

Stable bedding

The purpose of bedding is to provide a warm, dry, comfortable floor covering on which a horse or pony can lie down without knocking or injuring himself. It also takes some of the strain off the legs when a horse has to stand for long periods on a hard surface. Many different types are available. Whatever kind you choose, the bedding should be at least 15cm deep.

Straw is the dried stalks of wheat, barley or oats. It is cheap to buy, but some ponies like eating it and it can give them colic.

Aubiose is made from hemp. Sold in vacuum-packed bales, it is useful for horses and ponies who have dust allergies. It is expensive to buy.

Rubber matting is very expensive but saves time on mucking out. You need to use some bedding on top of it to soak up the wet.

Wood shavings are also sold vacuum-packed. Dust-extracted, they are good for horses and ponies with breathing problems.

Shredded paper is cheap, but some ponies are allergic to the ink in it. It is heavy to lift and unpleasant to handle when it is wet.

Far to walk
You may have to carry a field-kept pony's tack quite a distance.

Ways to keep a pony

You can keep a pony out in a field, in a stable, or partly in and partly out. Looking after a stabled pony is hard work and takes up a lot of time. It also costs more than keeping a pony in a field, but it is very convenient. A field-kept pony requires less looking after, but preparing him for riding takes longer. Many people think the ideal system is to stable ponies at night in winter and during the day in summer, and let them live out the rest of the time.

Winter field

In winter, fields can become very muddy and your pony may be wet and dirty most of the time. This is bad for his feet and legs. But field-kept ponies are less likely to suffer from coughs and breathing problems than stabled ponies.

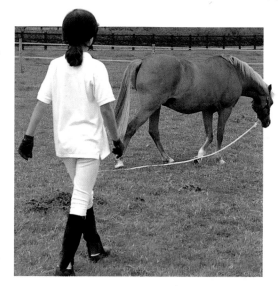

Catching a pony

Some ponies are difficult to catch, and some may try to pull away once caught. A trailing rope can be dangerous, so try not to let it go. It may be better to lead a difficult pony in a bridle.

Preparing for a ride

It is easy to prepare a stabled pony for riding. But before you can ride a field-kept pony you must walk to the field, catch him and then get him clean enough to tack up.

Regular feeding routine

When ponies are kept in stables they need feeding at regular times. Whether or not they have hard feed (page 25), they need hay fed in a haynet several times a day to give them the bulk food that grazing would provide if they lived out.

Mucking out

When you keep a pony in a stable, you have to muck it out thoroughly at least once a day, as well as removing droppings at regular intervals. This takes a lot of time and can be very hard work.

A stabled pony is entirely dependent on you for food and water.

Removing mud and stains

A stabled pony needs just a quick brush over before exercise to make him look presentable. This is called quartering (page 31). With a field-kept pony you must remove all the mud stuck to his coat. It is especially important to remove mud where the tack fits, or it may rub and cause sores.

Carrying water to the field

If the field does not have a trough that fills automatically, you will have to carry water to it every day. In warm weather, and if there are several ponies in the field, this can mean many trips to and fro with buckets.

American barn stabling

Many livery yards and riding schools now use American barn stabling. A long barn is divided into individual loose boxes with a central aisle. It is convenient in bad weather, but there can be problems with ventilation.

Where to keep a pony

If you are a new owner it is a good idea to keep your pony at a livery yard where you will have knowledgeable people to help you. Types of livery, and their charges, vary. Some riding schools charge less if they can use your pony for lessons. You may be able to rent a field and stable from a farmer, or be lucky enough to keep your pony at home.

Traditional loose boxes

Each loose box opens directly on to the yard, so the horses can see what is going on. An overhanging roof gives some protection from sun and rain to both the horses and the people working in and around the stables.

Planning a conversion

You may have a garage or outbuilding at home that can be turned into a stable. In most areas, your parents will have to apply for planning permission to change the use of the building, and they will have to submit plans to the local council. This can all take a long time.

A field and field shelter

If you only have a field in which to keep your pony, try to make sure there is some kind of shelter. This will protect your pony from the weather, as well as giving you a base in which you can put your belongings, groom the pony, tack him up, and feed him in winter. Do not leave tack in the shelter.

A farmer's field

A local farmer may let you rent a field and possibly a stable, too, though many do not like having horses on their land. If you do find one who is willing, it can be very useful because he will probably be able to supply you with hay and may even let you ride in some of his fields.

A stable of your own

If you want to keep a pony in your own stable at home, you need to plan well beforehand. The stable does not have to be perfect, or even conventional, but it must meet certain basic requirements and be safe and comfortable for the pony.

A converted building

You may be lucky enough to have a building at home that you can use as a stable. It must be in good condition, with a weatherproof roof and a sound floor. It must also be well ventilated.

A ready-made stable

You can buy a wooden stable as a kit and have it assembled at your home. You will need some kind of level, solid base on which to stand it. This will probably mean laying a concrete slab. You need to consider the site you will use carefully before you go ahead.

Planning a stable yard

If you are considering keeping a pony at home, remember you will need more than just a building in which to house it. Although you may only be planning to use one loose box, you will have to find space for storing feed, hay and bedding, and the latter two take up a lot of room. You must reserve a corner not too near the house for the muck heap. Tack and rugs must be kept somewhere, and if you do not have a paddock, you will have to find a field for a daily turn-out.

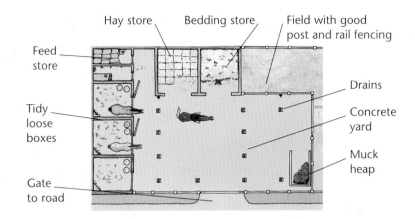

Hay store
Bedding store
Field with good post and rail fencing
Feed store
Tidy loose boxes
Gate to road
Drains
Concrete yard
Muck heap

A stable's requirements

When you are planning your stable, consider what it needs. First of all it must be large enough – about three metres by three metres for a pony. The doorway and ceiling must be high enough for him not to bang his head if he throws it up in the air. You will need a water supply nearby. Electricity is useful, but not absolutely essential. If you do have it, you must install light bulbs and switches where the pony cannot reach them.

Tying ring
It is useful to have tying rings both inside and outside the stable for tying up the pony and for hanging a haynet.

Automatic waterer
This needs to be plumbed in, but it will save a lot of time and effort carrying water buckets.

Manger
You can feed a pony or horse from a bowl or bucket standing on the floor, but a manger is less likely to become soiled.

Good drainage
A concrete or brick floor that slopes gently to a drain will provide good stable drainage. An earth floor can also be used.

Double doors
The open top half of the door allows the pony to look out. It should always be left open for ventilation.

Hopper windows
The top half of the windows should open inwards to let in air but not rain, and the glass should be protected by grilles.

Door bolts
Some ponies can undo the top bolts on their doors. A bolt with a lockable end prevents them from doing this.

Kick bolt
A foot-operated kick bolt on the lower part of the door saves having to bend down – useful when carrying things.

Stable management

Four-pronged fork

Wheel-barrow

Shovel

Yard brush

Shavings fork

Mucking out equipment

To muck out a stable you need a fork and a shovel for removing droppings and wet bedding, a broom for sweeping the stable and yard, and a wheelbarrow to carry the muck to the muck heap.

Stable management means the organization and carrying out of all the tasks that are centred round the stable. A large part of stable management is the daily routine of mucking out, feeding and watering, as well as keeping the stable and yard clean and tidy. Other jobs include the maintenance of equipment and checking feed and bedding stores.

Mucking out a pony's stable

A pony's stable needs a thorough mucking out once a day – removing the droppings and wet bedding – and skipping out – just removing the droppings – several times a day. The process is much the same for straw or shavings. Some people use a deep litter system, in which only the droppings are removed daily and fresh bedding is added.

Clearing up
Sweep any remaining muck and wet bits of bedding into a pile in the middle of the floor and use the shovel to put it all into the wheelbarrow. Continue sweeping until the floor is clean.

1 First remove all the obvious droppings on the surface with the shavings fork and put them in the barrow.

2 When you have done this, toss the shavings to the sides of the stable, removing any droppings that fall out of them as you do so.

3 Once you have removed the top shavings, those that remain on the floor will be wet. Scoop them up with the shavings fork.

4 Now the dry bedding is stacked round the sides and most of the wet has been removed, you can sweep the floor and shovel up the muck.

The bedding store

Shavings and straw bales must be stored somewhere. Straw must be stacked under cover, preferably in a hay barn, where air can circulate round it and prevent it from going musty. Shavings can be stacked outside, if possible under a waterproof cover.

Clean water

Horses and ponies should have access to clean water at all times. Whenever you visit the stable, check the bucket to see if it needs topping up. If the water is soiled, throw it away and rinse the bucket out well before refilling it. Every few days, scrub out the water bucket to keep it clean.

Water buckets are usually made of plastic or rubber.

A tidy muck heap

Try to keep your muck heap tidy. Ideally, you should divide it into three sections: one that you are using to tip the muck on each day, one that you are leaving to rot down, and one that has already rotted down to be used on the garden or disposed of elsewhere.

5 If possible, leave the floor to dry and air for a while before pulling back the shavings to lay the bed. Bank up the shavings round the walls.

6 You may not always need to add new shavings, but when you do, open the bale carefully, cutting the tape with scissors or a special safety yard knife that has a recessed blade.

7 Shavings are very tightly packed in their bales. It is often easiest to use the four-pronged fork to prise them out if you do not need to add a whole new bale to the bedding.

Choosing a field

A field suitable for grazing by horses and ponies should be level and well drained. It needs some form of shade and shelter, such as trees, hedges or a field shelter; secure, safe fencing; a clean water supply; safe access from the road; and a properly hung gate that can be locked if necessary. The grazing and hedges should be free from all kinds of poisonous plants.

Good fencing

Wooden post and rail is the best kind of fencing for horses and ponies, but it is expensive. Hedges with gaps in them and crumbling stone walls can be reinforced by a taut strand of electrified tape. Electric fencing works well if you keep it clear of the ground and check the supply regularly.

Good grazing

Horses and ponies thrive on a mixture of grasses, such as rye, timothy and meadow fescue, with some beneficial herbs and weeds such as dandelion, chicory and yarrow. Lush pasture fertilized with nitrates is not suitable for horses. The grazing must be properly managed.

Poisonous plants

You should check any field in which you are going to keep a pony for poisonous plants. Any you find should be dug up and burned. If the field is near a garden, check that the pony cannot reach plants such as rhododendron, laburnum, privet or other evergreen hedges. Most evergreens are poisonous.

Foxglove

Deadly nightshade

Ragwort

Hemlock

Horsetail

Water supply

A stream is not ideal because it may be polluted. A water trough that fills automatically is very useful, or you may have to use buckets. Both the trough and the buckets need scrubbing out regularly to remove the algae that build up.

Secure locks
Unless the field is well supervised, it is as well to keep the gate locked as a precaution against theft.

Safe gate

A properly hung and well-maintained gate that does not sag on its hinges, drag on the ground as you open and close it, or swing back and hit you as you go through, ensures you can lead your pony into the field safely. The gate may be made of wood or metal.

Signs of a bad field

A field that is covered in droppings and has more weeds than grass, with broken fencing and a gate held in place with string, is not suitable for a pony.

Uneven grazing
Tussocks of coarse grass surrounded by bare pasture usually mean that the field has been over-grazed. It needs topping and resting before being used again for horses or ponies.

Poached field
Poached means that the field is badly cut up and muddy. A poorly drained field with too many animals on it in winter quickly becomes poached, and is no use for grazing.

Too many droppings
A field covered in piles of droppings needs clearing and resting. The droppings kill the grass and contain many worm eggs. Grazing round these areas reinfests a horse.

Barbed wire fencing
Barbed wire should never be used for fencing where horses and ponies are kept. Many have been injured by it. The wire is especially dangerous if it is rusty or sagging.

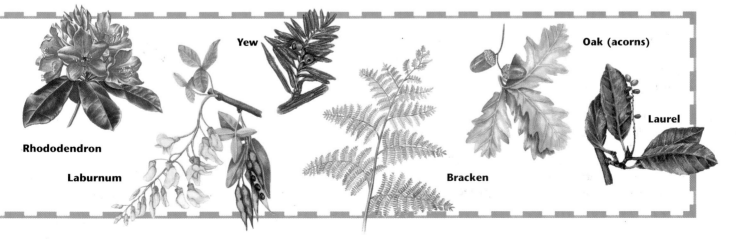

Rhododendron

Laburnum

Yew

Bracken

Oak (acorns)

Laurel

Looking after a pony's field

A pony's field needs a lot of attention to stay in good condition. Horses and ponies tend to graze parts of a field until they are bare, leaving tussocks of coarse grass and weeds untouched. Putting other animals in the field evens out the grazing, but it may also need spreading with fertilizer or lime, and rolling in the spring if it gets very churned up in winter.

Pulling up ragwort

Ragwort is a tall, poisonous plant with small, yellow, daisy-like flowers and ragged leaves. You should check a pony's paddock regularly for ragwort and pull or dig up any immediately. All traces of the plant should be destroyed. Put salt in the hole left after pulling it up to kill any remaining roots.

Removing droppings

Leaving droppings around not only damages the grass, but also encourages parasitic worms to breed. In a small field you should remove droppings every day with a shovel and a wheelbarrow or skip. This may not be practical if horses or ponies graze a large field, so the area should be harrowed instead to break up and scatter the droppings. The sun will then dry them out and kill off any worm eggs.

Topping a field

Once or twice each summer, a field needs topping, which is rather like mowing a lawn. A tractor pulls a machine that cuts down weeds such as docks, nettles and thistles, as well as the long, coarse grasses. This helps to stunt the weeds' growth and prevents them from scattering seeds. It also encourages new grass shoots to flourish, which provide more nourishing grazing.

Removing stones

Small stones can get lodged in a horse's or pony's feet and cause lameness. Large stones can be dangerous if horses or ponies gallop round a field, causing them to stumble, sprain tendons or even fall. It is a good idea to remove as many stones from your pony's field as you can.

Clearing rubbish

If a field is near a road, litter such as string (left) and plastic (right) may blow or be thrown into it. Plastic bags can kill a pony if eaten, and cans and glass bottles can cause severe cuts. String can become entangled round a horse's legs and also cause problems if eaten. You should check a field daily and remove any litter you find.

Turning out and catching

Turning out means putting a horse or pony out in a field. It is better to remove his headcollar to avoid any possibility of it getting entangled in fencing or hedges, but sometimes headcollars are left on ponies that are difficult to catch. If your pony gets excited at the thought of joining his friends in the field, try to keep him calm.

Turning out a horse or pony

As you lead your pony towards the field, other horses or ponies already there may gather inquisitively round the gate. If this happens, ask a helper to open the gate for you and shoo them quietly away so that you can take the pony into the field safely.

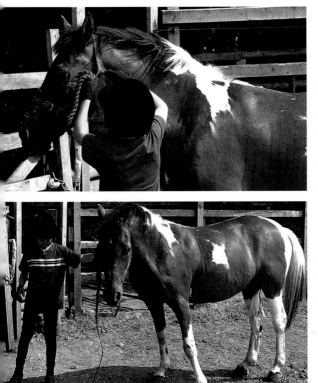

1 Lead the pony a few metres into the field after closing the gate behind you. Turn him round to face the gate and undo the buckle on the headcollar.

2 Slip the headcollar off his head gently and let him walk quietly away. If he gets excited and tries to whip round and gallop off, make sure you keep well out of his way.

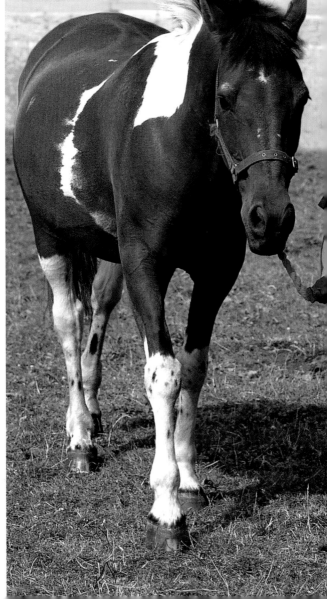

Carrots

Apple

Titbits
Although too many titbits can make a pony nip, giving him a treat when you visit him in the field can make him easier to catch.

Leading a pony

Ponies are usually led on the left-hand side. Hold the rope so that your right hand is near the pony's head with the palm facing down, and your left hand is near the end of the rope. Look straight ahead and walk level with the pony's shoulder.

Keeping hold of a pony

If the pony misbehaves, bring your right hand down to the end of the rope near your left hand. Try your best not to let go, but bring the pony round you in a circle. Never wrap the rope round your hands. If he pulls away, he will drag you after him.

Catching a horse or pony

Some horses and ponies are easier to catch than others. Approach a difficult horse with the headcollar behind your back and your hand outstretched holding a titbit or a bucket of pony nuts. If he runs away, do not chase him. Wait for him to come to you.

1 Walk towards the horse's shoulder from the front, holding out a titbit in your hand so that he can see it.

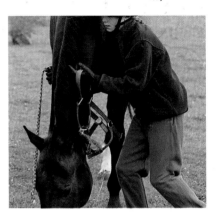

2 Give him the titbit and quickly slip the headcollar rope round his neck before he has time to move away.

3 Put the headcollar over the horse's nose, still keeping the rope round his neck in case he decides to wander off.

4 Reach under his jaw with your right hand and take hold of the headpiece firmly. Pass it over the top of the horse's head. Get hold of the headcollar's cheekpiece with your other hand.

5 Fasten the buckle of the headpiece so that it fits correctly – not too tight or too loose (see page 42). Tuck the end of the strap through the buckle to keep it tidy and out of the way. You can then lead the horse in from the field.

Feeding a pony

A pony's natural food is grass. He must eat a lot, taken in a little at a time, to provide nourishment. When we replace grass with hay and other food, we must try to copy this pattern.

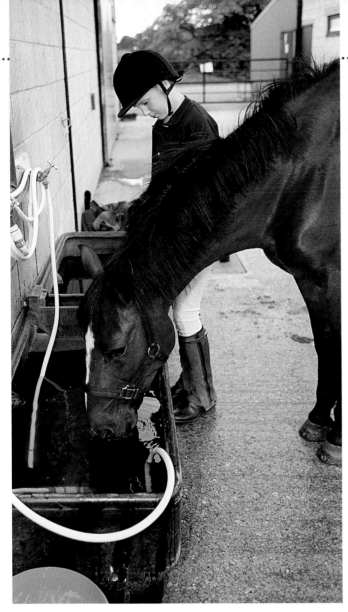

The rules of feeding

Horses' and ponies' stomachs are small and their intestines large. They need small quantities of food at a time, but a lot overall. This is how they eat bulk food such as grass or hay. But with hard feed (see pages 24–25) it is important that they do not get too much food in their stomachs at once.

Plenty of clean water

Clean water should always be available to a horse or pony. If, for some reason, it is not possible to allow him free access to water, then offer it to him at regular intervals before feeding. Watering after food can cause digestive problems such as colic.

Feeding rules

Feed little and often, rather than giving large feeds.

Only feed fresh food.

Match the amount of food to the work the pony does.

Do not exercise a pony immediately after feeding.

Introduce new foods gradually to a pony's diet.

Feed plenty of bulk food, such as good meadow hay.

Allow the pony to graze in the field for part of each day.

Feed a stabled pony something succulent, such as carrots or turnips.

Feed at regular times each day of the week.

Keep the manger clean.

A haynet keeps hay off the floor.

Regular feeds

It is best to give a pony hard feed rations in several small feeds evenly spaced during the day. Work out a routine that suits you and stick to it. Ponies do not understand the difference between a weekday and a weekend – they expect their food to appear at the same time every day.

Different types of feed

Horse and pony feed can be divided into two main types. Bulk feed – grass and hay – forms the major part of the diet. A pony may manage on that alone. If he works hard, he may need up to 30 per cent of his rations in the form of hard feed – also called concentrates.

Filling a haynet

Feeding hay on the floor is wasteful as the hay gets trampled and soiled. To fill a haynet, open it as wide as possible. Tear a slice of hay off the bale, pull it apart and push it into the centre of the haynet. You can get a rough idea of how much you are feeding by counting the number of slices you put in each time.

How much hay?
To be sure exactly how much you are feeding, weigh the filled haynet.

Tying a quick-release knot

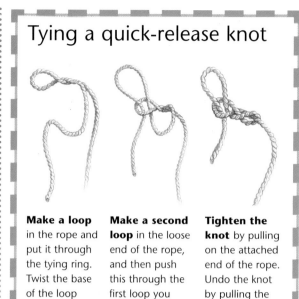

Make a loop in the rope and put it through the tying ring. Twist the base of the loop several times.

Make a second loop in the loose end of the rope, and then push this through the first loop you have made.

Tighten the knot by pulling on the attached end of the rope. Undo the knot by pulling the loose end.

Hanging a haynet

The haynet should be tied up quite high to prevent the horse from pawing at it and getting his foot stuck in it. Using a quick-release knot makes it easy to undo when it is empty.

1 Put the string of the haynet through the tying ring in the stable. Pull on the string to raise the haynet to the right height.

2 Loop the string through the rope mesh near the bottom of the haynet and take it back up to the tying ring.

3 Put the end of the string through the tying ring again and secure the haynet firmly with a quick-release knot.

Types of hard feed

Oats can make ponies unmanageable so it may be better to feed barley instead. Most hard feeds are best mixed with chaff (chopped hay and straw). Bran is used in mashes. Maize should be fed sparingly; sugar beet must be soaked before feeding. Pony nuts and coarse mixes are easy to feed.

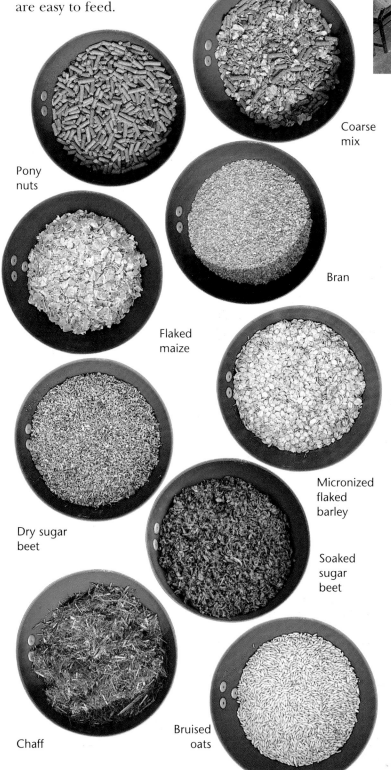

Pony nuts

Coarse mix

Flaked maize

Bran

Dry sugar beet

Micronized flaked barley

Soaked sugar beet

Chaff

Bruised oats

How to store feed

Feed must be kept in a cool, dry place and protected from rats and mice. In large stables, sacks of hard feed are emptied into metal feed bins, but for one pony, plastic dustbins make good substitutes. Hay must be kept in a dry barn where air can circulate round it.

Supplements and treats

All horses and ponies need salt, which can be provided by a mineral lick. In winter, feeding a little cod liver oil supplies essential vitamins. Ponies appreciate carrots, swedes and turnips both as treats and as winter feed. Apples are always very popular, but feeding too many can cause colic.

Mineral lick
Ponies enjoy licking and gnawing at mineral blocks both out in the field and in the stable.

Vegetable oils
Ponies need some fat in their diet and this can be provided by oils such as sunflower oil. About one tablespoonful can be added to a feed.

A diet for your pony

Horses and ponies may be 'good doers' or 'bad doers'. This means they can do well or even get fat on little food, or stay thin while eating a lot. An experienced horse-keeper will be able to work out a diet for a difficult horse or pony. With most ponies, it is better to be cautious about feeding, and if in doubt, give less rather than more. It is not kind to let a pony get overweight.

Working out your pony's weight

You can check your pony's weight with a weighband – a kind of tape measure. You pass the weighband round the pony's girth, and as well as reading the measurement, you can also read off his weight. You may need an assistant on the other side of the pony to check that the band is in the right position. You can also weigh the pony on a weighbridge.

Too thin or too fat?

Although they may both be the same height, a stockily built pony, such as a Highland, will carry much more weight than a thoroughbred type. So you have to assess a pony's fatness according to his type. It is important for the pony's health that he should be the right weight. A thin pony feels the cold. He uses his feed to keep warm, and may have little energy left for working. A fat pony puts a strain on his joints and heart.

A thin pony
If you can see a pony's ribs, if his hip bones stick out and his head looks too big for his neck, he is too thin. This may be the result of teeth problems, worms or lack of food.

A fat pony
When you cannot feel a pony's ribs or spine, and he has thick pads of fat over his shoulders and a large round belly, he is too fat. Fat ponies are prone to illnesses such as laminitis.

The perfect weight
A pony's outline should be smooth and rounded, without any obvious fat. You should not be able to see his bones, but you should be able to feel them if you prod with a finger.

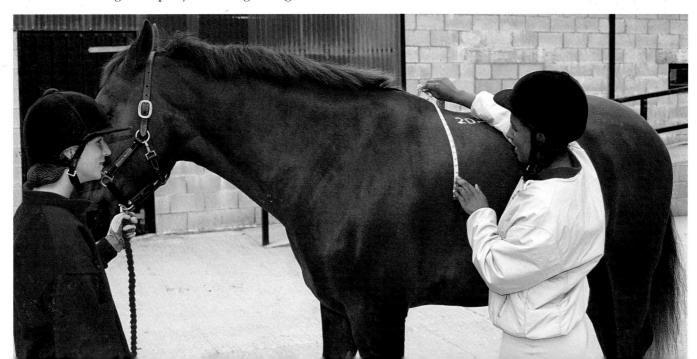

Measuring out

The only way you can be sure exactly how much food your pony is eating is to measure it out. Work out how much food he needs, by multiplying his weight by 2.5 and dividing the answer by 200, and write it down. Decide what proportion of this should be hard feed and measure it out for each feed.

Starvation paddock

Lush summer grazing can be too rich for some ponies, that become overweight and risk getting laminitis. Although it may sound cruel, they are best kept on an almost bare paddock, where they have to work hard to get grass to eat. An alternative is to stable them for most of the time and only let them out to graze for short periods.

Using a bucket muzzle

This is another way of stopping grazing ponies from eating too much. The muzzle has large holes at the front for breathing, and small holes underneath that allow a certain amount of grazing and let the pony drink. The muzzle is held in place by a head strap, which you thread through the rings on the headcollar.

Soaking a haynet

Ponies that suffer from dust allergies and have breathing difficulties are best fed hay that has been soaked in a tub of water for a short while. A plastic dustbin is ideal. Filled haynets can be very heavy when wet, so take care not to strain your back when lifting them out.

Weighing hay

It is a good idea to weigh filled haynets so you know exactly how much hay the pony is being fed. You can buy special spring balances, which you can hang in the feed room or on a gate, designed to weigh a filled haynet. If you are feeding your pony soaked hay, weigh it before you soak it.

Grooming a pony

Regular grooming keeps a pony's coat clean and shiny. It is also a good way of checking him all over.

Grooming equipment

Grooming means cleaning the pony's coat, tidying his mane and tail, picking out his feet, and keeping his eyes, nostrils, muzzle and dock area clean. Each of these tasks needs a particular piece of equipment. Using the right equipment for each part of the grooming process enables you to carry out the work more efficiently.

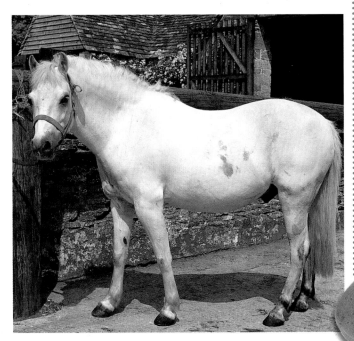

Why do I need to groom?

A fit, hard-working pony needs grooming every day to keep his skin clean and in good condition. But all ponies need brushing over regularly to remove dried mud and stable stains and keep the mane and tail tidy. This not only makes them look better, the ponies are also more pleasant to handle, and you and your clothes will stay cleaner.

Parts of the grooming kit

Ideally, you need all the different grooming aids shown here, but you could start with a few and build up gradually. To begin with, a dandy brush, body brush, metal curry comb, hoof pick and sponges are the most important things.

A dandy brush has stiff bristles and is used for removing dried mud.

A body brush has short bristles, designed to remove dust and grease from the pony's coat and skin.

A plastic or rubber curry comb is used to remove mud, loose hairs and stains.

A metal curry comb is pulled across a body brush to clean it. It is not for use on the pony.

A hoof pick, which may have a brush attached, is used to remove dirt and stones from the feet.

A water brush is used damp to lay the pony's mane and tail in place as a finishing touch.

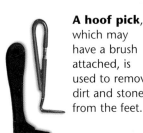

A mane comb is mostly used when pulling the mane and tail, to tidy them, and to separate the hairs before plaiting.

Hoof grease or oil is applied to the feet with a brush to give a smart finish for a special occasion.

One sponge is used to clean the eyes, nose and muzzle, the other to clean the dock area.

A stable rubber is a cloth used at the end of the grooming routine to remove any remaining traces of dust.

Grooming routines

A pony that lives out should only be brushed over lightly with a dandy brush to keep it tidy. A hard-working, stabled pony needs to be groomed thoroughly each day to keep its skin in good condition. Both the dandy and body brushes are used in the direction of the hair of the pony's coat.

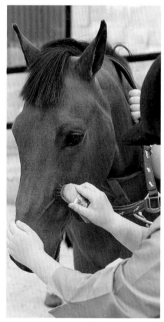

Clean the body brush on the metal curry comb after every three or four strokes.

1 For a thorough grooming, first tie up the pony. Starting at the top of his neck on the left-hand side, groom him all over using the body brush.

2 Then undo the headcollar and rope. Fasten the headcollar round his neck while you brush his face gently with the body brush or a special face brush.

3 Standing to one side of the pony, hold out the tail. Release a few hairs at a time and brush them with the body brush. Undo any knots with your fingers.

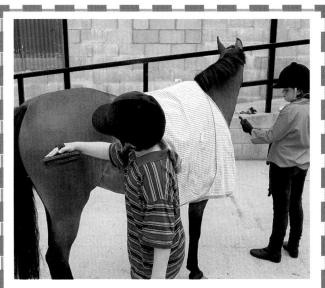

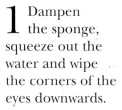

Sponging eyes, nose and dock

The corners of a pony's eyes, the nostrils, the muzzle, if it is dirty, and the dock area under the tail should be cleaned every day with damp sponges. Use different sponges for the face and for the dock, and remember which is which!

1 Dampen the sponge, squeeze out the water and wipe the corners of the eyes downwards.

2 Rinse the sponge and use it to clean round the pony's mouth and inside his nostrils.

3 Using a different sponge, clean the dock, including the underside of the tail.

Quartering

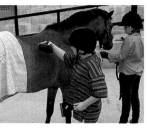

Quartering means a quick brushing over of a horse or pony to remove stable stains and shavings, or straw from the mane and tail. This will make him look tidy before going out for exercise. The real work of grooming is done after exercise. In cold weather the rug can be left over the forehand or quarters to keep the pony warm.

Fold back the rug over the pony's quarters while grooming his forehand. Do both sides, then fold the rug forwards over his forehand so you can groom his quarters.

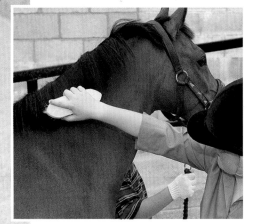

4 To clean the mane and remove any tangles, first brush it out thoroughly with the body brush. For a final neat finish, dampen the water brush and use it to lay the mane in place.

5 Although dried mud should be removed first, you can use a plastic or rubber curry comb instead of a dandy brush to remove any you may have missed on the legs.

6 The final step is to go all over the pony's body with a stable rubber. This is a cotton cloth that removes any remaining traces of dust and loose hairs, and gives a glossy finish to the coat.

Feet and foot care

Taking care of a horse's or pony's feet is one of the most important tasks an owner must carry out. A pony's feet must be sound. You should check and pick out a pony's feet before and after riding, and on non-riding days, do it at least once. You must also have them regularly trimmed by a farrier, and shod (pages 44–45) if you ride on rough tracks and roads.

When feet need attention

If a pony's feet have not been regularly trimmed, the horn of the hoof will grow long and ragged, and may split. When a pony does a lot of road work, the shoes will wear thin quickly and need renewing regularly. Overgrowth of the feet makes the shoe nails work loose, and the shoe may come off.

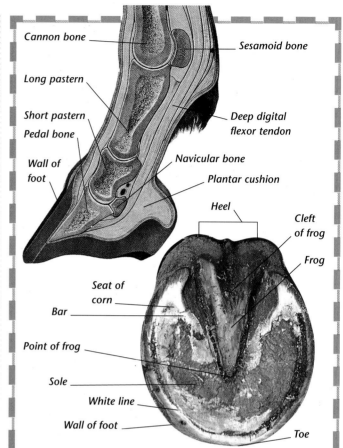

Cannon bone
Sesamoid bone
Long pastern
Short pastern
Pedal bone
Deep digital flexor tendon
Wall of foot
Navicular bone
Plantar cushion
Heel
Cleft of frog
Frog
Seat of corn
Bar
Point of frog
Sole
White line
Wall of foot
Toe

Structure of the foot

The outer casing of a horse's foot is made of insensitive horn composed of leaves, or laminae. Deep within the foot are the bones, which are held in place by sensitive laminae – fleshy leaves – which interlock with the outer laminae. It is the sensitive laminae that become inflamed in laminitis. The sides of the foot are called the wall, and the underneath is the sole.

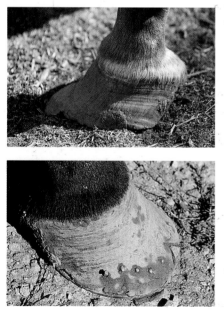

Overgrown hooves
If the hoof is allowed to become overgrown, the toes get too long and turn up, and the pony's weight goes back on his heels, altering the foot's balance. It can take a long time to correct this.

Raised clenches
When the foot has been neglected and allowed to grow too long, the clenches (the ends of the nails that hold the shoe on) rise out of the hoof wall. The pony can injure himself on them and may lose the shoe.

Stones lodged in the foot

Sometimes horses pick up small stones in their feet, which lodge in the grooves on either side of the frog. If they get wedged in, they can damage the foot, causing pain and lameness. You can remove them by digging them out with a hoof pick.

Picking up and picking out a foot

Be positive in your actions when you pick up a pony's foot. Slide your hand firmly down each leg so you do not tickle him. Always use a hoof pick from the heel of the foot to the toe, paying particular attention to the grooves between the frog and the bars, and to the cleft of the frog itself.

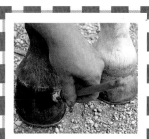

Oiling the feet

Applying hoof oil to a horse's feet makes them look smart, but you should not do it too often or it can prevent the hoof absorbing moisture. Pick out the feet and scrub off any mud with a water brush before you start. Let the feet dry, then apply the oil with a small brush. Hoof oil will not improve the quality of the foot's horn. Only a special diet can do this.

1 When you want to pick up and examine a pony's hind foot, start by putting your hand on the side of his hindquarters and sliding it down towards his leg.

2 Pass your hand firmly down the back of his hind leg. Do not be nervous when you are handling a pony or he will sense it and become nervous as well.

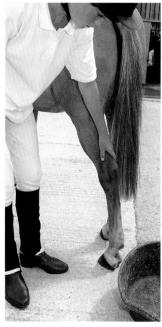

3 Continue down the back of his leg until you reach the hock. Keep your own feet away from the pony's in case he treads on you.

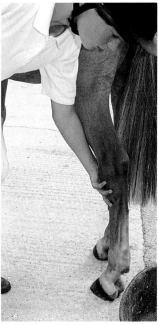

4 When you reach the pony's hock, bring your hand round to the front of his leg and move downwards over the cannon bone.

5 When you reach the fetlock joint, grasp it firmly and try to lift it, saying "Up" as you do so. Crouch – do not kneel – beside the pony.

6 Hold the pony's foot in one hand while you use the hoof pick from the heel towards the toe in the other. A skip is useful for the dirt.

Washing a pony

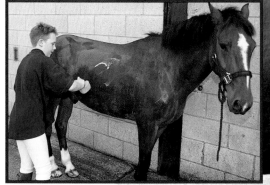

Only wash a horse or pony if it is absolutely necessary. Choose a warm, sunny and windless day. Washing removes much of the grease from a horse's or pony's coat. This makes them look clean and shiny, but means that until the grease builds up again they will feel the cold and have no protection against rain. They may need to wear a rug if the weather turns cooler.

Bucket of water

Shampoo

Sweat scraper

Sponge

Equipment for washing
Before you start, collect all the necessary equipment and put it where you can reach it easily.

Washing routine

It is important to keep the shampoo out of the pony's eyes, so when you are washing his neck and mane make sure his head is held up. Do not shampoo his face, just wipe it over with a clean, damp sponge.

1 Tie up the pony in the yard where the water can drain away. Fill a bucket with warm water and mix in the shampoo.

2 Dip the sponge in the water and rub it over the pony's coat in the direction of the hair. Cover the whole body, but not the head.

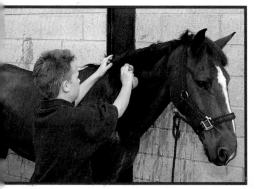

3 Wash the mane with the sponge, then rinse off all traces of the shampoo with another sponge and several buckets of water, or use a hose if the pony does not mind.

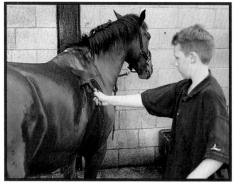

4 After rinsing, use the sweat scraper to remove the excess water, pulling it across the pony's body following the lie of the coat. If you do not have a sweat scraper, you can use the side of your hand.

5 Gently comb out the wet mane. If there are knots and tangles in it, undo them carefully with your fingers before combing. Do not try to drag them out with the comb or you will pull out the hairs.

Rinsing the saddle patch

In warm weather, when a horse returns from exercise with a sweaty saddle patch, you can hose him, if this does not scare him, or sponge off the sweat.

1 Wash the top of the tail with a wet sponge, warm water and shampoo, as you did the pony's body.

2 Rinse the tail in several buckets of clean water, swishing it round with your hand.

Washing a pony's tail

A pony's tail may need washing frequently, especially if it is a pale colour. Doing so will not chill the pony. Use a bucket of warm water and shampoo, lifting up the bucket to get as much of the tail in it as possible. Hold up the bucket with one hand while you squeeze dirt out of the tail with the other.

6 Rub an old towel all over the pony in the direction of the hair to dry him off as much as possible. Squeeze out the water from his mane in the towel and dry his neck underneath it. Do not forget to dry his legs and heels as well.

7 On a hot day the pony will dry naturally in the sun. If the sky clouds over, put an anti-sweat sheet or a cooler rug over him, and walk him up and down round the yard until he is dry, to prevent him from catching a chill.

Clipping a pony

Horses and ponies grow thick coats in winter. If they are worked hard they sweat a lot and lose condition. To avoid this, the areas where they sweat the most have the hair clipped off. A clipped horse or pony needs rugging to keep it warm when it is not working, even if it lives in a stable. Clippers must be handled with care, and the job is best done by an adult.

The hair is completely clipped off from the horse's head and neck.

Bandit clip
The horse is clipped all over except for his face, where the hair is left as protection from the rain. It is also a useful clip for a head-shy horse.

A bib clip runs in a straight line down the side of the neck.

Bib clip
The pony is clipped on the face, and the front of the neck, chest and shoulders. This clip is used for a horse or pony that sweats a lot on the neck.

Belly clip
The hair is removed from the belly and up between the forelegs. A variation is to clip the hair on the underside of the neck, too.

Hunter clip
All the hair is clipped except for the saddle patch and the legs, which are left unclipped for protection against sores and thorns.

Different types of clip

The different styles of clip reflect the amount of work a horse or pony is expected to do. Some hard-working horses are fully clipped; others have areas of winter coat left on for protection against the weather, saddle sores, cuts and thorns.

Trace clip
This is a popular clip for working ponies. Hair is removed from the underside of the neck, the belly and the lower part of the body.

Clipping equipment

Clipping machines are usually electrically operated. They have a number of blades, from fine to coarse, depending on the type of hair to be cut. The blades need oiling and cleaning regularly when in use.

Main clippers

Small clippers

The blanket area keeps the horse warm and dry.

The coat is cut in a semi-circle where the flank joins the quarters, following the line of the hair.

Blanket clip

This clip gets its name from the blanket area left unclipped on the back, which protects fine-coated horses against bad weather. The legs are also left unclipped. It is a useful clip for hard-working horses and is often used as an alternative to the hunter clip. With this clip, as with others, the areas to be left are marked out in chalk before clipping.

The clipping line at the top of the legs always slopes in a downwards direction from front to back.

The clippers are used with even pressure against the lie of the coat. They should move parallel to the skin without digging into it.

Blades for trimming coarse hair

Blades for trimming fine hair

Brush for cleaning clippers

Oils to lubricate clippers

Using the clippers

Clippers should always be used with a circuit-breaker to cut off the electricity if anything goes wrong. It is a good idea to wear rubber-soled shoes. The horse's coat must be clean and dry, and a haynet may help keep him quiet.

Other care
routines

Looking after a pony involves much more than
housing, feeding and grooming. Equipment
must be kept clean and in good order. His feet
need regular trimming and shoeing. He may have to
travel, and in extreme weather conditions, may need special care.

Checking the legs
When you get back to the stable, check the pony's legs for small cuts or any thorns he may have picked up, and feel for any heat or swelling.

Walking home
Provided you are not on a busy road, loosen the girth by one hole and let your pony walk on a loose rein to stretch his neck muscles.

At the end of a ride

Horses and ponies can get hot, sweaty and excitable during a ride. Always walk your pony the last kilometre or two home to let him cool off and calm down. At the end of a hard day, dismount, run the stirrups up, loosen the girth and lead him home.

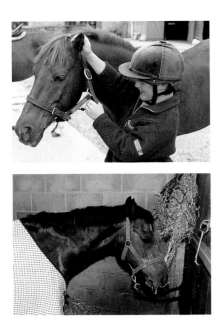

Rubbing the ears
A tired, wet horse may have cold ears. You can restore the circulation to the ears by grasping them at the base and pulling them gently through your closed hands.

All rugged up
If the pony is dry, brush off any mud before putting on his rug. If he is wet, thatch him by putting straw under the rug. Bandage wet and muddy legs over straw or gamgee.

Care after exercise

On your return home, unsaddle the pony, check him over and pick out his feet. Brush off any mud or sweat marks. In hot weather, you can sponge these off. Put on his rug, or an anti-sweat sheet, and if he is tired and thirsty, offer him half a bucket of tepid water. You can give him more later. Give a stabled pony a haynet before his feed. If he lives out, and is not cold or sweating, you can turn him out.

Choosing a rug

When a horse or pony has been clipped, he needs to wear a rug to make up for the loss of his winter coat and to keep him warm. On cold winter nights, he may need more than one rug, or an extra blanket under the rug. To be comfortable, the rug should be deep enough to cover the belly and should reach down to the root of the tail. Clipped horses are turned out in New Zealand rugs to keep off the rain.

Measuring for a rug

You need a long tape measure and an assistant to do this. Take the measurement from the centre of the horse's chest to the furthest point of his hindquarters. Rug sizes go up in about 7–8 cm increases, so you have to buy the nearest size.

Types of rug

Rugs are made in a bewildering variety of styles, shapes and materials. The latter may be natural, such as cotton, wool or jute; or synthetic, usually nylon or polyester. All rugs fasten across the front of the chest with either one or two straps. They are then held in place either by a roller, which goes across the horse's back and round his belly like a girth, or by crossed surcingles. These are sewn on to the right-hand side of the rug, and pass under the horse's belly to fasten on the left side, crossing over from front to back as they do so. There are special kinds of rugs for specific purposes, though most horses and ponies just need a stable rug and a New Zealand rug.

An anti-sweat sheet is a mesh rug used on a sweating horse to prevent chills as he cools down.

A stable rug keeps the horse warm indoors. It may be quilted or made of jute.

A New Zealand rug is waterproof and is used when the horse is out in the field in winter.

A summer sheet is a cotton rug used to keep the horse clean at shows and when travelling.

An exercise sheet is used to keep the horse's back warm during winter exercise.

A hooded New Zealand rug also keeps the pony's neck warm in bad winter weather.

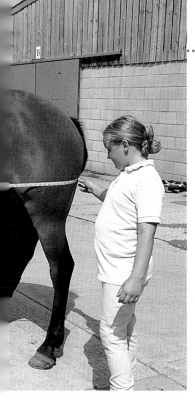

How to put on a rug

When you put on a pony's rug, do not fling it on to his back, lower it gently. Put on the rug well forwards of where it should lie so you can slide it back into place, thus leaving the pony's coat lying flat.

Crossed surcingles

These should be adjusted by sliding the buckles so they fit comfortably round the pony's belly. They do not need to be tight – there should be room for your hand to fit between them and the pony.

1 Tie up the pony. Carry the rug to him folded in half, with the back part folded forwards over the front part.

2 Holding the rug in both hands, lower it carefully on to the pony's back in front of where it should fit.

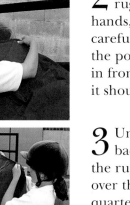

3 Unfold the back part of the rug and lay it over the pony's quarters. As you do so, check that it is lying straight.

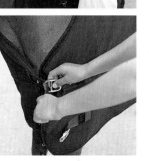

4 Fasten the breast straps, then slide the rug back until it lies in the correct position on the pony's back.

5 Undo the surcingles on the right side. Reach under the pony's belly for them from the left and fasten them.

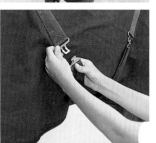

6 Finally, make sure that the rug does not press down on the pony's withers and that it is not too tight across his chest.

Roller

A rug may be secured by a roller, which fits quite tightly round the horse. An anti-cast roller has an arch in the centre to prevent a horse from getting stuck, or cast, when he rolls.

Anti-cast roller

Leg straps

New Zealand rugs are held in place by leg straps, one of which is looped through the other to prevent them rubbing. They must be fitted correctly.

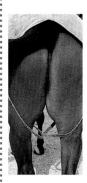

How to take off a rug

Tie up the pony. If the rug has a roller, undo it first and lift it off the pony's back. Make sure that the breast straps, surcingles and any leg straps are unfastened before removing the rug.

1 When you have undone the surcingles, tie them loosely in place on the right-hand side.

2 Undo the breast straps. Fold back the front of the rug to lie over the back.

3 Holding the folded rug with both hands, slide it backwards off the pony's quarters.

A pony's headcollar

Headcollars are made either of leather or webbing. They are used to lead a horse or pony, and to tie it up. Like bridles, they are made in three basic sizes – pony, cob and full-size. A very small pony may need a foal headcollar, which has a number of adjustable straps.

A good fit
This leather headcollar fits well. It fastens on the pony's left side, and the lead rope is clipped to the round ring under his chin.

Too small
This headcollar was made to fit a much smaller pony. The headpiece does not even reach far enough to meet the buckle on the cheekpiece.

Too large
This headcollar is much too large. The pony could pull his head back through it and escape, or get a foot caught up in it when grazing or scratching.

Checking the size

A headcollar needs to fit correctly in the same way as a bridle does. There should be room for you to insert two fingers under the noseband, and a hand under the throatlash. A headcollar that is too tight, especially if it is made of webbing, will rub and may cause sores over the pony's prominent nasal bones.

Fitting and caring for tack

Tack is a horse's or pony's saddle, bridle, headcollar and any other saddlery he may wear, such as a martingale. To do its job properly, it must fit well, be correctly adjusted and well cared for. Neglected tack is dangerous. It can give the pony sores and may break, leading to accidents.

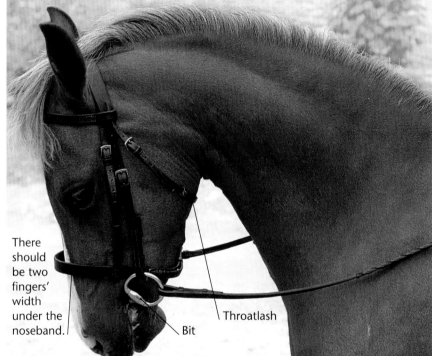

There should be two fingers' width under the noseband.

Bit

Throatlash

Well-fitting bridle

This pony is wearing a well-fitting snaffle bridle with an eggbutt snaffle bit. The browband is at the correct height so it does not pinch the pony's ears, the noseband and throatlash fit well, and the bit just wrinkles the corners of the pony's mouth.

Storing tack

Tack should be cleaned before it is put away. Bridles are hung on arched racks that do not bend the headpieces; saddles are supported on brackets fitted to the wall or on free-standing saddle horses.

You should see daylight between the saddle and the spine.

Saddle panel

How to clean tack

It is important to keep saddle and bridle leather clean and supple. If you do so it will last for many years. You should clean it each time you use it. To clean tack, you need a bucket of warm water, one sponge for cleaning off the dirt and grease, one sponge for saddle-soaping and a bar of saddle soap.

Wash the bit in clean water and dry it. Clean all the grease and mud off the bridle with a slightly damp sponge. Then dip the bar of saddle soap into the water and rub it on to your other sponge.

Fitting a saddle

Horses and ponies vary a lot in shape and size, and it is important that the saddle fits well. It must be the right width, and the panel stuffing must be even so the leather maintains a level contact with the pony's back. The saddle must not press on the pony's spine or the withers.

Rub saddle soap well into the leather, undoing fasteners so no parts of the bridle are neglected. Keep moistening the soap when you need more on the sponge. When you have finished, refasten all the buckles.

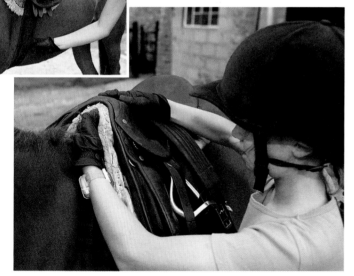

Wipe any mud off the stirrup irons with your cleaning sponge. Rinse the sponge, squeeze it as dry as possible, and clean the grease off the underside of the saddle, as well as any mud. Do not get the leather too wet.

Tacking up

Check that the numnah does not press down upon the pony's withers. You should be able to insert three fingers between the withers and the pommel of the saddle, and two between the girth and the pony.

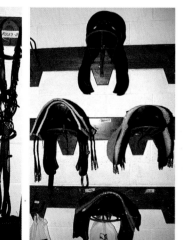

If you wet the sponge when you are using saddle soap, you will have too much lather. Moisten the soap instead. Rub the sponge all over the saddle. Don't forget the girth straps and stirrup leathers.

Shoeing a pony

Ponies' and horses' feet grow like your fingernails, and need trimming every six to eight weeks to keep them in good condition. Shoeing prevents the feet from wearing down too quickly when the pony is exercised on hard surfaces like roads. The person who trims and shoes a pony is called a farrier. Most farriers have mobile forges and travel round to work at their clients' premises.

Hot shoeing

When a shoe is heated in a furnace before being tried on a pony's foot the process is called hot shoeing. Because the horn of the foot is insensitive, like your nails, the pony cannot feel it. A pony may need new shoes each time the farrier visits, but if the shoes are not very worn, the farrier will simply reshape them and use them again.

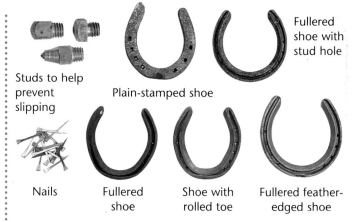

Studs to help prevent slipping

Plain-stamped shoe

Fullered shoe with stud hole

Nails

Fullered shoe

Shoe with rolled toe

Fullered feather-edged shoe

Types of shoe

Most horses and ponies wear fullered shoes, which have a groove running round them to give a better grip in the mud. Farriers can make special types of shoes to correct most horses' and ponies' foot problems, as well as shoes for various kinds of work.

1 Using the buffer and mallet, the farrier cuts the nail ends, or clenches, that hold the shoe on to the foot.

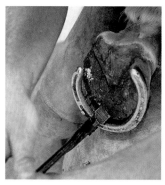

2 When he has cut the clenches, he levers off the shoe with pincers, starting at the heel and moving towards the toe.

3 He neatly cuts away the excess growth of the horn all the way round the foot using the hoof cutters.

8 He then tries the shoe in place on the hoof. The heat burns the horn, causing it to smoke.

9 When he is satisfied, he cools the shoe in a bucket of water before starting to nail it on to the pony's foot.

10 He hammers the nails through holes in the shoe to hold it in place, starting at the toe and working back.

Fitting studs

So that horses and ponies can be ridden across country in wet or muddy conditions, studs are sometimes screwed into special holes in the heels of their shoes.

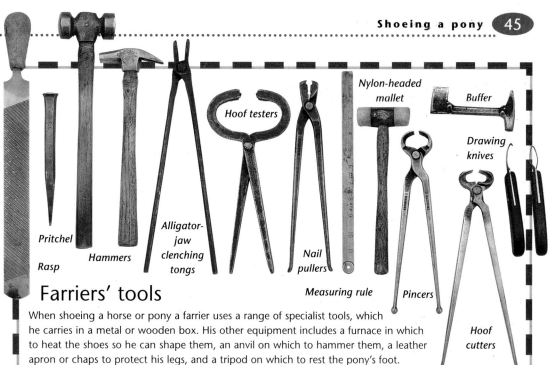

Pritchel

Rasp

Hammers

Alligator-jaw clenching tongs

Hoof testers

Nail pullers

Nylon-headed mallet

Buffer

Drawing knives

Measuring rule

Pincers

Hoof cutters

Farriers' tools

When shoeing a horse or pony a farrier uses a range of specialist tools, which he carries in a metal or wooden box. His other equipment includes a furnace in which to heat the shoes so he can shape them, an anvil on which to hammer them, a leather apron or chaps to protect his legs, and a tripod on which to rest the pony's foot.

4 He tidies up the wall of the foot, the sole and frog, cutting off any ragged bits with a drawing knife.

5 Using the rasp, he makes sure that the weight-bearing surface of the foot is absolutely smooth and level.

6 He then heats the shoe in an oven called a furnace until it is red-hot, handling it carefully with pincers.

7 He hammers the hot shoe into shape on the anvil, still holding it with the pincers and reheating it if necessary.

11 The nails come out of the side of the hoof and the farrier twists off their ends with the claw of a hammer.

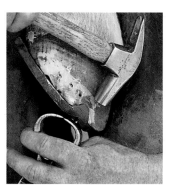

12 Resting the shoe on the pincers, he hammers down the projecting nail ends to form the clenches.

13 With the foot on a tripod, he uses the rasp to smooth the ends of the clenches and the rim of the hoof wall.

14 The finished foot should look neat and even, with six or more nails holding the new shoe in place.

Travelling safely

If you wish to take part in riding club events, shows or gymkhanas you will need to transport your pony in a horsebox or a trailer. Once they get used to it, most horses and ponies do not mind this, and learn to brace themselves against the movement of the vehicle. In doing so, however, they may knock their legs, so they need to wear protective clothing. They also wear rugs to keep them warm and clean.

Storage
Water can be carried in a large plastic container.

Providing food and water

While travelling, a haynet will keep your pony happy. Store hay for your return inside the box rather than hanging it outside where it may be contaminated by exhaust fumes. On a long journey, you may also need to take water.

Travel boots
Shaped and padded travel boots fit round the lower part of the pony's legs and are held in place by several Velcro straps.

Boots and bandages

To protect a horse's or pony's legs you can either use special travel boots or bandages. Travel boots cover the legs from the knee or hock to the coronet at the top of the hoof (pages 60–61). If bandages are used, the horse or pony may also need to wear kneecaps and hock boots to cover his joints.

Travel bandages
Used over felt padding, these are put on in the same way as first-aid bandages (see pages 54–55).

1 Start by laying the bandage across the top of the pony's tail, leaving the end sticking up.

2 Then take the bandage under the tail and bring it round to the top, holding the end.

3 After a couple of turns of bandage round the tail, fold down the end you left out.

Bandaging a pony's tail

The top part of a pony's tail is bandaged before travelling to stop him rubbing it against the back of the box. Bandaging also lays the hairs flat and keeps the tail tidy. The bandage needs to fit quite firmly. To prevent it becoming soiled, the bandaged tail can then be folded up and secured with an elastic band.

Travel essentials

Your pony's tack, plus saddle soap, sponges, etc., to give it a final clean

Your riding clothes if you are going to a show

Food and water – for both you and your pony!

Any documents you may need – tickets, entry forms, etc.

First-aid kit for you both

Loading your pony

Most ponies will walk up the ramp of a horsebox or trailer quite happily, but if yours is unhappy about it, let him take his time. If he still hesitates, ask a helper to put one of his front feet on the ramp. He will then usually walk in without a problem. Food may help.

Walk confidently up the ramp.

Don't pull your pony.

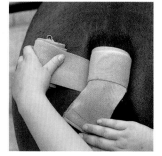

Reward him when he goes in.

Ready to go

A single pony in a double trailer travels better on the side nearer the centre of the road. Tie him up quite short, and put the bar or breeching strap across. You can use the other compartment for luggage.

Unloading your pony

Untie the pony, leaving his rope through the ring so he thinks he is still tied up. If your trailer has a front ramp, put it down, then remove the bar or strap. Lead him down the ramp slowly. To unload backwards, ask a helper to stand at the side to keep the pony moving straight back.

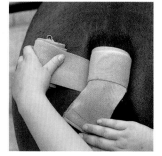
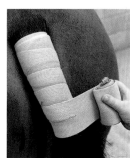
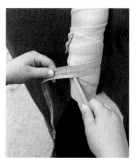

4 Wrap the bandage over the folded-down end to prevent it from slipping.

5 Continue bandaging down the tail until you reach the end of the dock.

6 Cross the strings, take them round to the back and cross them again.

7 Tie the strings round the bandage in a neat bow to hold it securely in place.

8 Fold a layer of bandage over the bow to stop it from coming undone.

Removing a tail bandage

To remove the tail bandage, unfold the part over the bow, untie the strings and slide the whole thing off in one movement, laying the hair flat and smooth as you do so. Roll up the bandage from the strings end with the strings folded inside.

Summer and winter care

Extremes of temperature and weather may mean that a horse or pony requires special care. In hot summer weather, horses seek shade, and an escape from the flies that can make their lives miserable. In the depths of winter, a field-kept pony will have little to eat, and the ground may be muddy or frozen. The water supply may freeze up, too. We have to solve all these problems.

Preventing sunburn

Horses and ponies that have pink noses can suffer from sunburn. It particularly affects stabled animals, who may stand with their heads over the stable door for hours in the sun. You can protect them from sunburn by applying a sunblock cream made for use on human skin.

Fly fringe
A fly fringe can be fitted over a headcollar, or worn on its own. As the horse moves, the strings keep flies out of his eyes.

Fly repellent
A number of products are available to help ward off flies. Most are poured on to a cloth and wiped on the pony's coat. Some ponies do not mind spray products.

Coping with fly nuisance

Horses and ponies that suffer greatly from flies are best stabled in the daytime and turned out at night. If this is not possible, then fly fringes, or netting veils, which cover most of the face, can help. Horses provide their own protection by standing in pairs nose to tail, each swishing the flies off the other's face.

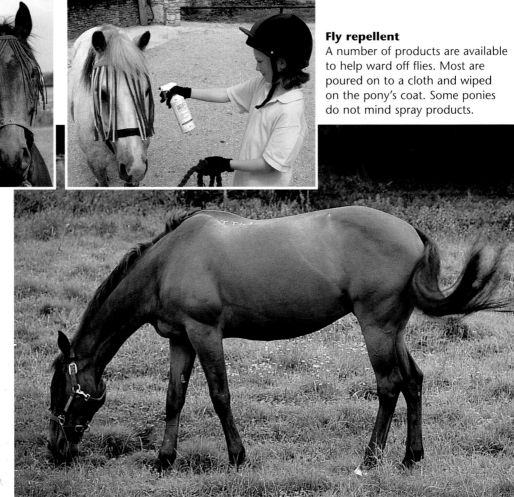

Leg and foot care

In winter, a horse's or pony's legs and feet need special attention. Constant exposure to wet and mud can cause mud fever (page 57), so it is worth trying to protect them from this. Riding on ice is dangerous because your pony may fall, but you can ride in snow if you grease his feet.

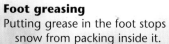

Foot greasing
Putting grease in the foot stops snow from packing inside it.

Leg greasing
Applying Vaseline or liquid paraffin to a horse's lower legs and heels helps keep the mud and wet off them.

Keeping warm
A clipped horse or pony will stay warm in the coldest weather if he has sufficient food and if he wears a thick enough rug. It is better to add an under-blanket or another rug for warmth than to shut the top half of his stable door.

Breaking the ice
In severe weather, the water in field troughs and even in stable buckets will freeze. To ensure that your pony has enough to drink, you must break the ice several times a day. If possible, use warm water for topping up because this will refreeze less quickly.

Essential winter care

Native ponies can live out without rugs all winter if they have enough to eat. Depending on the weather, the pasture, the pony and his work, he will need some hay and possibly hard feed from mid-winter to spring.

Health care

Horses, and especially ponies, are hardy animals. Provided you follow a few simple rules, they stay healthy. However, things can go wrong, so you need to know how to cope when they do.

Pricked ears
Although ears laid back are a sign of bad temper rather than ill health, pricked ears show that the pony is interested in what is happening. His ears move to catch the slightest sound.

Bright eyes
A pony's eyes should be bright and clear. The pupils should dilate in the dark and contract in bright light. The eyes should not run, though a small amount of dirt may collect in the corners.

Dry nose
A horse's nose should be dry. Some animals that are allergic to dust may have a slight, watery nasal discharge. But thick mucus, especially if greenish or yellow, is a sign of infection.

Other things to check

A healthy horse or pony should be neither fat nor thin. Sticking-out ribs and a pot belly are signs of worms, as is a cough. The horse's breathing should be relaxed and regular – noisy breathing may be a sign of lung disease or dust allergies. At rest, the horse should feel warm, with cool feet and legs. His droppings should be formed and should just break on reaching the ground.

Signs of good health

A healthy pony has bright eyes, a shiny coat, a keen appetite, and is interested in everything that goes on around him. Ponies are inquisitive, and will come and investigate what you are doing. Out in a field, they stay together in a group. A pony that keeps away from the others may not be well.

Signs of ill health

If a pony stands with his head down looking unhappy, if his eyes are dull and his coat is in poor condition, he may be ill. Pinch his skin between your finger and thumb. It should spring straight back into place. If it does not, the pony may be dehydrated (lacking water).

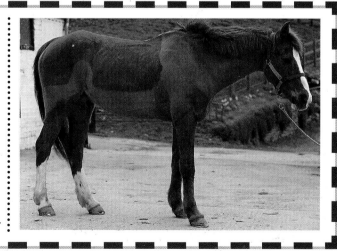

Full of life

Although horses and ponies in a field spend most of the time grazing, they will play and gallop around, especially if they are young. This helps them get exercise and also keeps them fit. They only sleep for about four hours a day, and one always stands guard while the others lie down. Horses and ponies can also doze standing up.

Health routine

Regular worming and vaccination are essential to help keep a horse or pony in good health. It is important to know your pony's usual pulse, temperature and respiration (breathing) rates, and also to be able to recognize its normal behaviour. Being aware of these things will help you to spot anything that is wrong and remedy it very quickly.

The vet watches the pony move. If he drags a hind toe, this may indicate lameness in that leg.

Checking the pulse and respiration

Feel for the pulse with your fingers just under the pony's jawbone. Count the number of beats you feel in one minute. It should be 35 to 45 when the pony is resting. The pony's respiration rate is 10 to 20 breaths a minute at rest.

Checking legs

A pony's legs should feel cool and be free from swellings. By running your hand down each leg in turn every day, you will be able to feel any swellings or heat, which may indicate an injury even if the pony does not seem lame.

Trotting in hand is the easiest way to check for lameness.

Lameness

If you walk or trot a horse or pony on hard ground, such as a yard, it is possible for someone watching to tell on which leg he is lame. With foreleg lameness, a pony will nod his head as the sound front leg hits the ground.

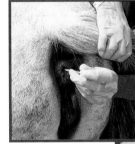

Keep a firm hold of the thermometer for two minutes before you withdraw and read it. Make sure you do not let go!

Taking the temperature

If you think your pony may be ill, ask an adult to help you take his temperature. The normal temperature for a horse or pony is between 37.5°C and 38.5°C. Grease the bulb of the thermometer and insert it gently into the pony's anus.

Worming

Horses and ponies need worming every four to eight weeks. The wormer may be a powder, which you sprinkle in your pony's food, or a paste, which is squirted on to his tongue with an applicator. Ponies don't seem to mind the taste. You should ask an adult to help you worm your pony.

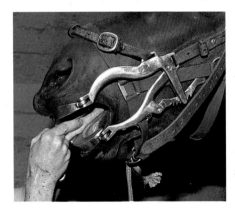

Care of the teeth

Horses' and ponies' back teeth often wear unevenly, making the mouth uncomfortable. It is a good idea to have them checked each year by a vet or an equine dentist. He or she will rasp smooth any sharp edges, using a gag to keep the pony's mouth open and avoid being bitten.

Gauze

Wound powder

Iodine

Antiseptic solution

Petroleum jelly

Gamgee

Poultice

Bandages

Cotton wool

Worming paste

Round-ended scissors

Thermometers

First aid

It is useful to know how to carry out basic first-aid routines to help you deal with a horse's or pony's minor injuries and problems yourself. But if a pony shows obvious signs of illness, or is lame or badly injured, you should ask the advice of a knowledgeable adult, as it may be necessary to call out the vet. Prompt veterinary attention can prevent a problem from getting worse.

First-aid kit

It is a good idea to have a first-aid kit handy. Keep it in a clean, dry place and check it from time to time. If you use any of the contents, replace them so they will be there the next time you need to use them in an emergency.

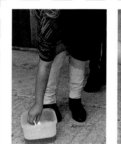
Make sure you use clean cotton wool.

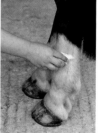
Clean the wound from the centre out.

Preventing infection

Thorough cleaning of a wound will prevent infection and help it to heal quickly. Clip off the surrounding hair. Pour warm water into a clean container and add some antiseptic. Dip clean cotton wool into the solution, squeeze it out, and use it to clean the wound. Use more cotton wool until the wound is clean. If the wound bleeds a lot, or is near a joint or tendon, call out the vet.

Hosing the legs

Hosing an injured leg with cold water can reduce swelling and pain. Ask a helper to hold the pony and just trickle the hose on his leg to start with. Then hose the leg for about 15 minutes, stop, let it warm up again, and then repeat the procedure once or twice more.

Leg bandages

Bandages may be used to hold a dressing in place, to support injured or swollen legs and to keep cold, wet legs warm. Bandages are put over a layer of padding called gamgee. When bandaging the legs, crouch – do not kneel – beside the pony.

Applying wound powder

You can treat minor cuts and scratches with antiseptic wound powder, which you puff on to the wound after cleaning it. As well as helping to prevent the entry of infection, wound powder helps to keep flies away.

1 Bandage any dressing in place, then wrap gamgee round the leg. Cover the coronet and make sure the gamgee is kept flat.

2 Start applying the bandage just below the knee or hock. Hold the end in place until you have secured it with a few more turns.

1 Cut the poultice to the size you need and soak it in either hot or cold water. Squeeze out the water while keeping the poultice flat.

2 Place the poultice over the sole of the pony's foot and start to bandage it in place. It is easiest to use a stretch, self-adhesive bandage.

3 Bandage in a figure-of-eight shape round the hoof. When you have finished, tape thick cotton wool or a bag round the foot.

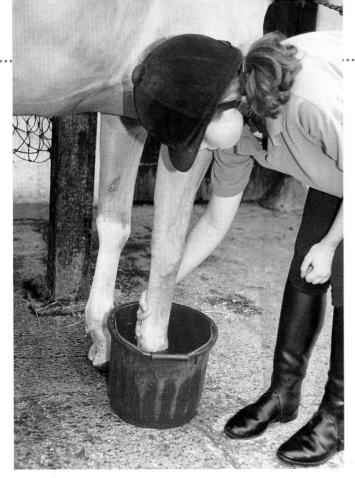

Tubbing a foot

Tubbing means putting a horse's foot and lower leg in a bucket of warm water containing Epsom salts. This is used to help draw out infections of the hoof. The horse needs to stand with his leg in the bucket for 10 to 15 minutes, preferably twice a day. Unless you know the horse is quiet, ask an adult to help.

Applying a foot poultice

Poultices may be used hot or cold. A hot poultice is used to draw out infection from a wound or abscess, a cold one to reduce swelling, for example, when the foot is bruised. You can buy chemically prepared poultices, made of cotton wool and gauze.

Finished poultice bandage

3 Work down the leg and over the fetlock and pastern until you reach the top of the hoof. Try to keep the tension even as you work.

4 When you reach the coronet, apply the bandage in the opposite direction and work your way back up the pony's leg.

5 By the time you have got to the end of the bandage, you should have arrived back at the place on the leg where you began.

6 Secure the bandage with Velcro straps or tapes. Tie the tapes neatly on the inside or the outside of the pony's leg.

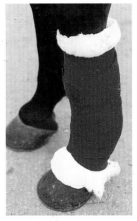

7 The finished bandage should be firm but not too tight. You should be able to see a layer of gamgee at its top and bottom.

Common ailments

Even the best cared-for horse or pony will occasionally suffer from a minor ailment. Once you can recognize what is wrong, you can carry out simple treatment. Look out for signs of abnormal behaviour in your pony, for areas of sore, rubbed skin, for lumps and swellings, and for any signs of lameness. Laminitis and colic are the most serious problems you are likely to encounter. Both can be caused by a pony over-eating.

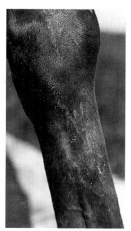

Bot-fly eggs

Little yellow specks on a pony's lower legs in summer are bot-fly eggs. Ask an adult to scrape them off with a knife. If the pony licks the eggs, bot larvae develop in his mouth and stomach. Worming with ivermectin in early winter destroys the bot-fly larvae.

Rubbing mane

Even if they do not have sweet itch, many horses and ponies rub their manes and tails in summer, which looks unsightly and causes soreness. Rub in benzyl benzoate, or protect the horse with a special lightweight hooded rug and a fly screen for the face.

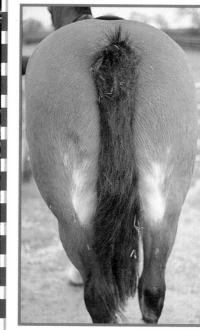

Sweet itch

Sweet itch is the name of an allergy to the bite of tiny midges, which causes some ponies to rub themselves raw to try and get rid of the irritation. The mane and tail are usually affected.

The midges mostly bite early in the morning and at dusk, so the best way to avoid sweet itch with a susceptible pony is to stable him at these times.

Benzyl benzoate, from the chemist, rubbed into the roots of the mane and tail, helps relieve the symptoms of sweet itch.

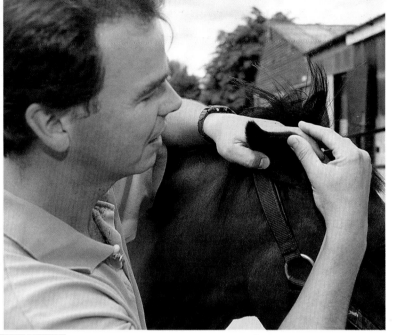

Ear plaques
Areas of white skin in the ears, called plaques, are harmless and do not need treatment.

Looking for mites
You may not see the mites, which are tiny, but thick brown wax in the ears gives them away.

Problems with a pony's ears

Shaking of the head, rubbing of the ears and a discharge from the ears are all signs of ear problems. The symptoms may simply be the result of ear mites (tiny parasites), but they could also indicate an infection. If you suspect something is wrong with a pony's ears, have them examined by a vet.

Symptoms of colic

Colic is a common digestive problem, and can be very serious. Affected ponies often roll, but then do not shake themselves afterwards. They may lie down and get up again frequently. If badly affected, they will sweat and be in obvious pain. If you see signs of colic, call out the vet immediately.

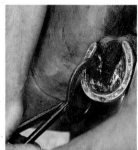

Mud fever
Sore, cracked heels need treatment by a vet.

Hoof testers
Check for laminitis by applying pressure.

Swollen leg
This swelling on the lower leg might be the result of a knock or a sprain. Hosing the leg (page 54) may help.

Swellings in the legs

Swellings can be caused by ligament or tendon injuries; bruising; splints, which are bony enlargements; arthritis and other conditions. They may feel hard or soft, there may be heat in the leg, and the pony may be lame. It is generally best to seek veterinary advice.

Mud fever and laminitis

Mud fever is a winter problem; ponies that eat too much rich summer grass can get laminitis, a very painful inflammation of the hoof. It usually affects the front feet, which feel hot, and the pony may be lame. If a pony has symptoms of laminitis, get him in from the field and call the vet.

Caring for a sick pony

A sick or injured pony that is confined to a stable likes to follow his normal routine as far as possible. Provided he is not too ill, you can give him a light daily grooming. Keep him warm with rugs if necessary, and make sure he always has clean water to drink. If he cannot go out at all, pick him a few handfuls of grass to enjoy each day, as long as the vet allows it. Never feed a pony lawn trimmings.

Giving a pony medicine

Medicines come in different forms – powders, pills and liquids. Powders and liquids can be mixed in the feed. Putting them in a tasty, moist food, such as soaked sugar beet, helps to disguise the taste. Pills can be crushed between two spoons and fed in the same way. Liquids may also be dropped on to the horse's tongue or inside the lower lip, or squirted into the mouth with a syringe.

Hide a pill or capsule in a slice of apple. Cut a slit in the apple and push the pill down into it so the pulp of the fruit surrounds the pill and masks the taste.

Powdered medicine can be sprinkled on to a slice of bread with treacle. Fold the bread to hide the powder and tear or cut it into bite-sized pieces.

Convalescence

A horse or pony confined to a stable for a long time gets very bored, especially when he is feeling better. Divide his hay ration into several smaller nets to keep him occupied. Visit him frequently, and bring him titbits. Some horses and ponies like a radio left on for company.

Things to play with

If the horse or pony is allowed to move around, he may enjoy playing with a horse football. You can buy several types of horse toys, which are designed to be safe, and impossible for the horse to puncture if he bites or kicks them.

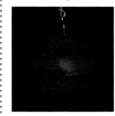

Stable toys include hanging balls, on which you can smear treacle.

Feline friend

When a horse or pony has to be confined to the stable for long periods and he has no other equine friends around, he may appreciate the company of a friendly household cat or dog, especially if you cannot visit him as often as you would like.

Grazing on the lawn

If your pony cannot go out into the field but is allowed out of his stable, spare a few minutes each day to give him some in-hand grazing, provided the vet allows it. It is also a good way of keeping the lawn trimmed!

The road to recovery

Once the pony has recovered from his illness, you must get him fit before he can resume normal work. Start by giving him gentle exercise. A good way to do this is with a few minutes' in-hand walking each day, gradually increasing the time and distance. If you are leading him on a road, keep him well into the side, and walk in the direction of the traffic. Position yourself between the pony and the traffic.

Wear a hard hat
and gloves when leading
a pony on the road.

A pony should wear
a bridle when being
led on the road.

Wear light-coloured
or reflective clothing

Points of a horse

The points of a horse or pony are the visible parts of his anatomy. Each has a name, which you will find useful to learn, as they will help you understand magazines and books you read, and instructions you may be given when you take riding lessons. By becoming familiar with these terms you will learn more about horses and ponies, and be better able to talk to other people interested in horses. You will be able to discuss pony care, and talk over any problems with a vet.

Conformation

Conformation means the way in which a horse or pony is put together. It varies according to type and breed, but the body should look in proportion. A small head; large, clear eyes; sloping shoulders and pasterns; a good circumference of bone below the knee; a short back and powerful hindquarters are considered good conformation.

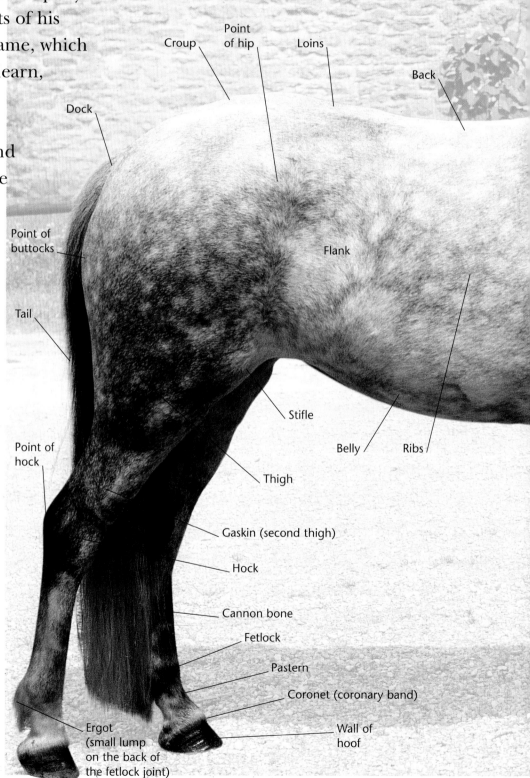

Croup

Point of hip

Loins

Back

Dock

Point of buttocks

Flank

Tail

Point of hock

Stifle

Belly

Ribs

Thigh

Gaskin (second thigh)

Hock

Cannon bone

Fetlock

Pastern

Coronet (coronary band)

Ergot (small lump on the back of the fetlock joint)

Wall of hoof

Poll
Neck
Crest
Mane
Shoulder
Withers

Ear
Forelock
Forehead
Eye
Cheekbone
Nose
Nostril
Muzzle
Mouth
Chin groove
Jaw
Cheek
Throat
Jugular groove
Point of shoulder
Breast
Elbow
Forearm
Chestnut
Knee
Heel

Skeleton

The skeleton is the bony framework around which a horse's body is built. The skull protects the brain, and the ribs protect the heart and lungs. The leg bones support the horse's weight and the joints allow him to move. Muscles, attached to the horse's bones by tendons, produce movement.

Internal organs

The horse has a large heart and lungs, which enable him to perform fast movement over a period of time. His brain is small. The spinal cord runs down from the brain through the spine. From the spinal cord, nerves radiate to all parts of the body. The stomach is small, but the intestines are about 30 metres long.

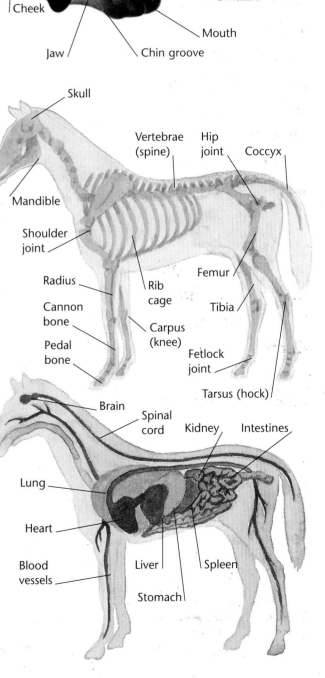

Skull
Mandible
Shoulder joint
Radius
Cannon bone
Pedal bone
Vertebrae (spine)
Hip joint
Coccyx
Femur
Rib cage
Carpus (knee)
Tibia
Fetlock joint
Tarsus (hock)

Brain
Spinal cord
Kidney
Intestines
Lung
Heart
Blood vessels
Liver
Stomach
Spleen

Glossary

American barn stables

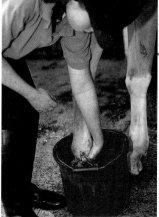

Tubbing the foot

You may not understand all the words you come across as you read about horses and ponies, and get to know more about their world. This list explains what some of them mean.

American barn A kind of stabling in which a large barn is divided into several **loose boxes** on either side of a central aisle.

anvil A shaped iron block on which a **farrier** works metal to make horseshoes.

bit The part of a bridle that goes in a horse's mouth – usually made of steel.

body brush A short-bristled brush used for removing dirt and grease from a horse's or pony's coat.

breeching strap A strap across the back of a trailer that stops a horse from moving backwards.

bulk feed Grass, hay or other **forage** that forms the main part of a horse's diet.

cantle The back of a saddle.

chaff Chopped hay and straw, which is mixed with other feed to stop horses eating it too quickly.

clenches The ends of horseshoe nails that are hammered down to hold the shoe in place.

clippers Hand-held machines with many small blades used for **clipping** a pony's coat.

clipping Removing a horse's or pony's winter coat to enable it to work without sweating excessively.

coarse mix A type of prepared **hard feed** in which various ingredients are mixed together.

cob A short-legged, small, stocky horse, usually with a quiet temperament.

colic Abdominal pain. Colic can be very serious and needs veterinary attention.

concentrates The grains such as oats and barley that make up **hard feed**.

conformation The overall shape and proportions of a horse or pony.

coronet (coronary band) The part of a horse's leg immediately above the hoof.

curry comb a) A metal comb on a wooden handle used for cleaning a **body brush** when grooming. b) A plastic or rubber version that can be used on a horse or pony to remove mud and loose hairs.

dandy brush A wooden-backed brush with long, stiff bristles used for removing dried mud and for grooming a field-kept pony.

deep litter A system of stable management in which only the droppings are removed in daily mucking out, and fresh bedding is placed on top of the old.

DIY livery A way of keeping a horse at a **livery** stable where the owner visits each day and does all the work.

dock The area under the top of a horse's tail, and the top part of the tail itself.

eggbutt snaffle A snaffle **bit** in which the mouthpiece is joined to the rings by thickened, smooth pieces of metal to prevent the bit from pinching the corners of the pony's mouth.

farrier A professionally qualified person who shoes horses and trims their feet.

fetlock The joint on the lower part of a horse's leg just above the foot.

field shelter An open-fronted shed in a field that provides horses and ponies with some protection from the weather.

forage Food for a horse or pony, especially grass, hay and **haylage**.

frog The V-shaped structure in the sole of a horse's foot that acts as a shock-absorber.

full livery Keeping a horse or pony at a **livery** stable where the stable staff carry out all the work involved.

fullered shoes Horseshoes that have a groove running round the underside to give a better grip.

gamgee Cotton wool lined with gauze, used as a padding under leg bandages.

girth a) The strap that goes round a horse's belly to hold the saddle in place. b) The part of the horse round which the girth fits.

grass livery Keeping a horse or pony out at grass at a **livery** stable.

grazing rotation Grazing a field with cattle and sheep after horses to even out the pasture and prevent the build-up of worm eggs.

halter A piece of equipment consisting of a noseband and headpiece, put on a horse's head to lead it.

hands The units used to measure a horse's height. One hand equals 10cm.

hard feed Corn, pony nuts, coarse mixes and so on, fed to a horse in small quantities.

haylage Vacuum-packed, partly dried hay. It is dust-free and fed to horses with breathing problems.

headcollar Similar to a **halter**, with a **throatlash** and a strap that joins the throatlash to the noseband.

horse An equine animal 14.3 **hands** (150cm) high or taller.

horsebox A vehicle used for transporting horses and ponies from place to place.

New Zealand rug

Ragwort

Clenches on a shod horse

Sweat scraper

Clippers for clipping
a horse

in-hand Leading a horse
or pony while on foot.

kick bolt A foot-operated
bolt on the bottom part of
a stable door.

laminitis A painful
inflammation of the inside of
a horse's feet, usually caused
by over-feeding.

livery Keeping a horse
or pony on someone else's
premises, and paying them
to look after it for you.

loose box A stable in which
a horse is free to move about.

lungeing Exercising a horse
on a long rein attached to a
special **headcollar**. The
horse is asked to walk, trot
and canter in circles.

manger A container, usually
fixed to the stable wall, in
which the horse's food is put.

martingale A piece of tack
designed to stop a horse
from throwing its head
up too high. A standing
martingale runs from the
noseband to the **girth**; a
running martingale from
the reins to the girth.

mud fever A condition in
which the heels and lower
legs get sore and cracked.

muzzle The area round
a horse's mouth.

native pony A breed such
as Exmoor, Welsh or Highland
that was bred on the moors
and mountains of Britain.

near side The left side of
a horse or pony.

New Zealand rug
A waterproof rug held on
with special straps worn by
a horse living out in a field.

numnah A saddle-shaped
pad used under a saddle.

off side The right side of
a horse or pony.

part livery A **livery** system
in which part of the work is
done by the stable staff and
part by the owner.

pastern The part of a
horse's leg between the foot
and the **fetlock** joint.

plaiting A pony's mane
may be plaited for a show.

poached ground Ground
that is cut up and muddy.

pommel The front part
of a saddle.

pony An equine animal up
to 14.2 **hands** (147cm) high.

pony nuts A balanced mix
of prepared feed, also known
as horse or pony cubes.

poultice This is a dressing
used to draw out infection
from a puncture wound.

pulling a mane and tail
Pulling out long hairs to
neaten the appearance.

quartering A quick
brushing over done before
exercising a horse or pony.

quick-release knot A
knot that can be undone
quickly by pulling one end
of the rope.

ragwort A yellow-flowered
plant that is highly poisonous
to horses and other animals.

roller A broad band that
fastens round a horse's belly
to hold a rug in place.

rolling A horse or pony
lying on its back with legs
kicking in the air, rolling
from side to side.

saddle soap A substance
that cleans, nourishes and
preserves leather.

shavings Wood shavings,
usually dust-extracted and
sold in vacuum-packed bales
for animal bedding.

skip A container for
shovelling droppings into
when mucking out.

stable stains Marks on
a stabled horse caused by
lying in dirty bedding.

strapping Thorough
grooming of a stabled horse,
done after exercise.

studs Metal pieces screwed
into the heels of a horse's
shoes to prevent it slipping.

surcingle A strap attached
to a rug to fasten it round
a horse's belly.

sweat scraper Used for
removing water from the
horse's coat when washing
it or sponging it down.

sweet itch An allergic
condition causing a horse
to rub its mane and tail.

tack All the pieces of
saddlery used on a riding
horse or pony.

thatching Putting straw
under a wet horse's rug to
help it dry without getting
the rug wet.

thoroughbred A breed
of horse registered in the
General Stud Book. All
racehorses are registered
thoroughbreds.

throatlash A strap on a
bridle or **headcollar** that
goes round a horse's throat.

topping a field Cutting
down weeds and long, coarse
grasses to improve grazing.

trailer Horse transport
towed behind a vehicle. It
may hold one or two horses.

tubbing a foot Soaking
a horse's or pony's foot in a
bucket containing a warm
solution of Epsom salts to
draw out infection.

turning out Letting a horse
or pony out in a field.

vaccination An injection to
protect a horse from diseases
such as 'flu and tetanus.

water brush A short-
bristled brush used damp
to lay the mane and tail in
place when grooming.

weighband A tape
wrapped round a horse's
girth from which you can
read off its weight.

withers The bony ridge at
the base of a horse's neck.

worming Giving medicine
to kill parasitic worms.

Index

HORSE AND PONY WEB SITES
www.hartpury.ac.uk
(information on courses run and
events held at the centre)
www.talland.net
(information about the school
and the courses run there)
www.pony-club.org.uk
(official Pony Club web site)
www.bhs.org.uk
(official British Horse Society
web site)
www.ilph.org
(International League for the
Protection of Horses web site)

Kingfisher would like to thank:
Everybody at **The Talland School
of Equitation**, especially the
Hutton family and Patricia Curtis.
Everybody at **Hartpury College
Equestrian Centre**, especially
Margaret Linington-Payne.
Models: Tom Alexander,
Anna Bird, Emily Brady, James
Cole, Emily Coles, Patricia Curtis,
Sam Drinkwater, Amelia Ebanks,
Naomi Ebanks, Helen Grundy,
Sarah Grundy, Simon Grundy,
Emma Harford, Brian Hutton,
Sophie Kuropatwa, Thomas
McEwen, Alasdair Nicol, Andrew
Poynton (farrier), Max Thomas
(farrier), Camilla Tracey, Ayako
Watanabe, Laura Wilks and
Sawako Yoshii.